AF322643

THE RISE OF DWAYNE 'THE ROCK' JOHNSON

THE RISE OF DWAYNE 'THE ROCK' JOHNSON

SCARLETT NORA

CONTENTS

CHAPTER 1

Disclaimer

The content in this book is intended for informational and entertainment purposes only. While every effort has been made to ensure the accuracy of the information presented, the author and publisher make no representations or warranties of any kind, express or implied, about the completeness, accuracy, reliability, suitability, or availability with respect to the content of this book.

The views and opinions expressed in this book are those of the author and do not necessarily reflect the official policy or position of any individual, company, or organization mentioned. Any resemblance to actual persons, living or dead, or actual events is purely coincidental.

This book is not intended to defame, libel, or slander any person, company, or organization. All references to individuals, companies, products, and brands are for illustrative purposes only, and no affiliation with or endorsement by them is intended or implied.

The author and publisher disclaim any responsibility for any actions or outcomes resulting from the application of information contained in this book. Readers should seek professional advice or conduct their own research when making decisions based on the content provided.

CHAPTER 2

Introduction

What do you get when you mix Dwayne Johnson with a little bit of charisma? The People's Champion, "The Great One", The Rock. If you smell what I'm cookin', it's the rise of Dwayne 'The Rock' Johnson from the wrestling ring to being the box office king, creatively known as The Rock. He's a multi-talented personality with a brilliant career graph.

A living legend in professional wrestling, Dwayne 'The Rock' Johnson has established himself in the world of sports entertainment. Former WWE wrestler, with 15 years of dedication to the company and numerous championship reigns, has made him a substantial fortune. Following his father Rocky Johnson's footsteps, Dwayne initially followed a career in the sports of football which was later abandoned. He belongs to the notorious Anoa'i wrestling family and has mixed Polynesian/Samoan and American origin. He had won his first WWE match at the 1996 Survivor Series. As per reports of Riches, Dwayne John has a calculated net worth of $440 million. "Following his father Rocky Johnson who was a pioneer: the first African American Georgia Heavyweight Champion, the first Black Mississipi Heavyweight Champion and the first Black World Tag-Team Champion." Dwayne Tahjai Johnson, former professional wrestler who is presently into acts, is predominantly renowned by his ring name the Rock. He was first signed in by the professional wrestling promotion World Wrestling Federation (WWF) now WWE in 1996 and has made a comeback in numerous promos and specially in 2018, and 2007. Johnson had even signed a developmental contract in 1996 and was directly sent to the Memphis Championship Wrestling (MCW), till he got promoted in the following year and bagged the WWF Intercontinental Champion. Johnson's wrestling milestones include the WWE Unified Champion and the WWE Royal Rumble Champion. At the peak time of his career, he was also known as 'the most-electrifying man in sports entertainment'.

CHAPTER 3

Early Life and Wrestling Career

Dwayne Johnson, universally adored for the roles he has portrayed on the big screen, is a colossal figure of a man. As many people think back onto his exploits in the movies they have seen him in over the years, it's easy to forget the twists and turns he took to find success in Hollywood. Johnson was born on May 2, 1972, in Hayward, California. His lineage is a mix of Samoan and African-Canadian descent, and his father, Rocky Johnson, had an influence on his career choice early on. His father was a professional wrestler and was inducted into the WWE Hall of Fame in 2008. Rocky Johnson's wrestling career had a major impact on Dwayne in more ways than one. Growing up, Dwayne and his family moved around quite often due to Rocky's wrestling career. A new school awaited Dwayne on an almost annual basis, and for someone who would grow to be over 6-foot-5 and physically gifted, he often found himself on the wrong end of bullying. That said, his experiences bouncing around schools ended up serving a purpose.

As a senior at Freedom High School in Bethlehem, Pennsylvania, Johnson tore his ACL and was forced to give up his scoring role in the high school football team. Despite receiving offers from various universities to play football and a potential career as a professional footballer, Johnson followed in his father's footsteps. Wrestling was in his blood, and he spent countless hours in different territories, learning the ins and outs of it. Rocky's relationship with several McMahons made it easier for Dwayne to transition over to the WWE (World Wrestling Federation at the time). Initially, he was asked to follow the path of his father and grandfather before him by playing strictly off his heritage, and he became Rocky Maivia, tying together the first names of his father and grandfather. The WWE audience, however, did not react kindly to the "face" version of Maivia. The wrestling world eventually felt the dissatisfaction of the WWE Universe, and Dwayne Johnson was eventually allowed to play a "heel" version of Rocky Maivia, completely altering course as a character.

Childhood and Family Background
Early Days
Raised in Hayward, California by his black wrestler father, Rocky Johnson, and Samoan mother, Ata, Dwayne spoke candidly about his heritages' influences on his life: "My Samoan family is a very spiritual family. They take a lot of pride in it, and a lot of pride in the family, a lot of pride in knowing where they come from and how they got to that place. My mom's hugely proud of it. My dad was also a guy who was just filled with a lot of pride: pride for his family, pride for sport, pride for how he carried himself. So I took a little bit from both of them." Dwayne spent a fair portion of his childhood traipsing the back halls of various venues, following around his father, who was often on the road performing in matches all around the world.

The Johnson family was well-known in the wrestling community. Ata, a former professional wrestling promoter, was Mickey

Rourke's first manager in the biz; she also once saved the Rock from getting into a fist fight in front of Little Richard. Between the many memorable characters he met during these formative years, Dwayne also spent a significant portion of his childhood watching his father scrap in the ring, sometimes coming home with over 50 stitches from various matches. Due to long stretches away on tour, the father and son didn't get a whole lot of time together as his father competed in matches all over the country and beyond. In fact, Dwayne watched his father compete live for the very first time in 1976 when he accompanied him to what would prove to be the penultimate match of Veronica, California-LA based female wrestler Ethel Brown's 42 years in the squared circle. Successful old high call to the corporate ring.

Transition to Wrestling

Plan your trip. Dwayne decided to exit the glitzy world of football for a career in wrestling. There were several reasons for this transition. One, wrestling was in his veins – it had helped shape his destiny. His grandmother, Leah Maivia, Dwayne's grandfather Rocky Johnson's wife, is the sister of Peter Maivia. Another factor was his curiosity. He had watched his dad in the ring and it had fascinated him. Was he tough enough to follow in his father's footsteps and grapple with some of the most talented athletes in the business?

New ring. New name. It was well and good before we officially posted the website link to Dwayne's new site "The Rock." Business was very easy to handle as personal Juda Benjamin was well respected locally. As far as small-time wrestling went, it seemed like there wasn't much that Dwayne couldn't accomplish. Even though he went off on his defeated path, he built many reputable bridges with promotions around the southern small-time wrestling circuit. Many of those names and faces are still heard of today such as "The Hardy

Boyz," Jeff and Matt Hardy, also Rhino, and Rikishi Phatu. Now known as Rocky Maivia, the wrestling superstar failed to capitalize on his family tree.

Dwayne found college football to be uninspiring and uneventful. "I didn't want to look back and regret not giving it my all," he admits. "This may surprise some people, but I didn't have an easy go of it. When I was coming out of college, I had all of one scholarship offer – to play football. Unbelievable! It seems like everything was so difficult because I played for a school – the University of Miami – that others viewed as a powerhouse." In addition, it was hard to get noticed over and above some of the local football heroes as there were just so many of them. It was an uphill struggle, but Dwayne gave it his all and made every minute count. He was desperate to fulfill his dreams. He wanted to play football, but never lost sight of his other passion – wrestling. During his junior and senior years at college, he decided to play football full throttle. Although the damage to his body was extensive, he wouldn't have missed it for the world. So, fired up again, he decided to crawl out from his temporary abyss and tackle his dream of wrestling – even if that meant starting from scratch. From this emerged 'Rebirth: My Rise from the Ashes'. Written by Dwayne 'The Rock' Johnson, this motivational saga has fired the little zest of wrestling in many a reader. With the help of author Joe Layden, Dwayne, in 2000, wrote "The Rock Says...". A mixture of biography and autobiography, "The Rock Says..." chronicles Johnson's life as a professional wrestler and his early years as a child growing up in New Zealand and the United States. This is the perfect book for any fan of The Rock. "The Rock Says..." has 19 chapters, is 292 pages long, walks the reader in all areas of Dwayne's life.

CHAPTER 4

Transition to Acting

Followed by his inclusion in this wrestling fraternity, Johnson commenced his venture in the world of acting after he agreed to portray a supporting role which was cast opposite Brendan Fraser in The Mummy Returns, which was shot in 2001. Though he made a cameo performance solely in the initial show in the trilogy, the portrayal of The Scorpion King was to pivot this wrestler's on-screen career. This marked Johnson's venture in the acting sector, offering him a pay of $5.5 million, which easily marked him as one of the highest paid debuting actors in history.

After having created an identity for himself in the wrestling sector, Johnson marks his transition from the ring to the silver screen and enters Hollywood. However, the competitiveness in the acting realm as well as his lack of experience behind the camera posed challenges, and many were skeptical of his crossover. In addition, a wrestler that jumps the ropes to go directly into the acting world, bypassing other wrestlers that went directly into films. However, in an interview, Dwayne Johnson explains that he essentially now has plenty of time, especially considering the fact that he is about to become a father. While he participated in wrestling for his youth, Montreal hosted the first "The Rock" competition, and Montreal's F1 race was also associated with Dwayne Johnson. He got his chance.

Yet a starting budget is another reason for making this decision. Even after the WWF has become an honorary representative of the professional sports association, Johnson says it is extremely difficult to find sponsorships and commercials in the United States. However, his associations have certainly faded, but still exist to this day. At the time, no company wants to be the face of an advertising campaign. Dwayne Johnson marked abandoning his dream of becoming a professional football player because he was mostly devoid of the possessive sector.

Debut in Hollywood

Branded to be the Rock, WWF's original creation, Johnson decided to take a break in 2003 from the wrestling ring to fuel up a new aspiration, which is to become the actor he once dreamed of being. His cropped beard, a 6'5" height, a footballer's body, the people's eyebrow, and the Rock's signature gimmick were not a part of his transition. His debut as an actor was to play the role of Mathayus the Scorpion King in 2001's The Mummy Returns. Because of his torn left Achilles tendon he suffered during a match in his final run for WWF, Johnson received criticism from some parties in the acting and wrestling realms for accepting the movie without auditioning for it. Then, while the Scorpion King was released in 2002, negative feedback was given on the performance of the Scorpion King.

This film, in spite of that, was remarkably successful at the box office and resulted in a spin-off sequel, The Scorpion King, released in 2002. It was at this point in time that Johnson approved of his debut and recognized that this would be the road ahead for him. He fought most auditions for several years and sometimes so aggressively that he was told by those in the casting industry that they had been forced to say it then, but he had reached the point where he showed off his auditions with such talent that he managed to comfortably show off his discerning attitude and interpretation. His only disadvantage at the time was his 'Rock' image as he sought to transition from the world of professional wrestling to that of an actor. Speaking in the WWE production of 2002 ring, Johnson informed Vince McMahon of his decision to renew his career and form the acting fraternity.

Breakthrough Roles

With acting opportunities coming slowly at first, it wasn't until 2001 that Dwayne 'The Rock' Johnson took on his first leading role in The Scorpion King, landing him a spot in the record books (which we'll get to later). Using this momentum to further his acting career, the former pro-wrestler went on to be cast in a variety of memorable and critically acclaimed roles, featuring in projects such as Gridiron Gang, The Rundown, and Southland Tales. Despite it taking a few more years, Johnson managed to prove to Hollywood that he was a box-office king when The Scorpion King became a box office hit, bringing in $165.3 million and overtaking Jet Li's 2000 film Romeo Must Die to make Johnson officially the actor holding the world record for the highest paycheck for a first-time leading role with $5.5 million.

Arguably one of his most successful roles to date, Dwayne Johnson decided to slow down on the wrestling to focus on acting and decided to expand on the character that originally made him a household name. For the first time, Dwayne Johnson was credited as Dwayne 'The Rock' Johnson in the opening credits and ultimately picked up $5.5 million upfront, making this his most successful performance as an actor thus far. Dwayne's other memorable roles include the popular and beloved Disney animation Moana, in which he voiced the character Maui, Jumanji: Welcome to the Jungle, and Snitch. It was slowly but surely that Dwayne 'The Rock' Johnson rose to stardom and affirmed himself as a prominent figure in the acting and film industry today.

CHAPTER 5

Brand Building and Business Ventures

In a sport often criticized for short-sightedness and lack of strategic vision, Dwayne Johnson emerged as a virtuoso. He knew how to give people what they wanted, creating a 'brand' that would transcend his niche. As the 1990s gave way to the 2000s, it was financial advice the Rock was dishing out to fans in the car or health sections of the bookstore. Then sales of his wrestling-promoted video game, WWE Smackdown, bore testament to his promotional clout.

While still just 30 and winning world titles in front of 60,000 in big city football stadiums, Johnson was already making bold inroads away from the ring and into the business world. He would start the process of bringing the wrestling together with the larger media world by setting up his own TV production company and hiring an ex-WCW producer. Not surprisingly, the Rock would be the first client and his autobiography the first project. In July 2002, Smackdown drew a 5.0 TV rating. Two weeks later, the Rock's autobiography debuted at the top of the New York Times bestseller list. In another parallel media move, the Rock struck a deal with the Microsoft Network website to create the official site for his book complete with interactive games. As well as producing, acting, and wrestling, the Rock would enter the stock market game with as much gusto. In 1998, at the height of his wrestling stardom as the World Wrestling Federation champ, Dwayne Johnson made his first investment in the stock market. Hitting the headlines again, on the day he won his sixth world wrestling title on 1 July 2002, it was announced that Johnson's film company would list publicly on the US Nasdaq stock market under the fancy ticker symbol of 'NWENF' (New Line Wrestling Entertainment).

Establishing the 'Rock' Brand

Many of us today know Dwayne Johnson from his movie career, but he was originally considered a direct-to-video actor that did a lot of work in the action genre. From the time he first entered Total Nonstop Action in 2004, he was immediately a larger than life personality, as he was in World Wrestling Entertainment. In fact, Dwayne Johnson did business simply as "The Rock" until 2008, when he went back to being Dwayne Johnson for his acting career.

As part of Total Nonstop Action, then known as TNA Wrestling, he built himself as "The Rock brand." It was an attempt to convince fans that as "The Rock" from WWE, he was a world-class wrestler. The company even helped him sue WWE for the rights to use the name, as it was his identity as an athlete. But should Johnson have the right to use "The Rock" as an actor in Hollywood? His character reached such heights in WWE that despite walking away from the business completely for years, younger fans checking out his old clips think he still works there. His version of his character "The Rock" was as famous as Mike from Jersey Shore, and people who hadn't seen all that much wrestling knew the "If you smell what the Rock is cookin'" catchphrase.

Dwayne Johnson, to use his actual name, gets attention, but "The Rock" brand means box office gold. Reach up and take a look.

What Rock's been cooking is every second of "The Rock" brand, and in seven years, Dwayne Johnson has given us every single reason to come and see one of his films.

Building 'The Rock' brand, Johnson thought a lot about how to use his 'Rock' nickname in different ways before adopting a rich man's rap star persona in WWE. When he first signed up with the company, he visualized himself becoming the "Rocky" of the 21st century, marrying wrestling, acting, and business into a singular path through life. With WWE, and mostly without them when that time ended, he's done exactly that. Though having John Cena at "Rocky's" side didn't hurt.

Johnson did a lot of things early on to develop the "The Rock" brand, including a clothing line worn by little kids in roughly 2006. That's before he became known for having a lot of business ventures, largely tied up with 'The Rock' brand. Most wrestling fans recognize "The Rock" as part of it, too, as everything from a host on "The Tonight Show" to a three-decade successful movie career is considered "The Rock" brand.

The Rock universe was not an entirely new concept when Johnson started using it outside of WWE, but over time it became pretty unique to him. Rocky Johnson and Tony Atlas were known as the "Soul Patrol" in the 1980s, a title that was still being used by other teams in both WWE and TNA when Johnson made his debut. But as the business changed and those with the rights realized they could make money off "Soul Patrol" Johnson, WWE's lawyers managed to get control of a plethora of "The Rock" trademarks. This helped signify a shift; that Johnson the actor could use "The Rock"'s momentum and give us "The Rock" contemporary. Thus came the clothes, then the tequila, and finally the XFL.

Earlier this year, The Hollywood Reporter and Forbes covered how Johnson has managed to establish the "The Rock" brand as its own thing. Head over to Google and The Rock universe, not the WWE universe, will catch your eye first.

Business Ventures and Investments

Dwayne Johnson launched his company, Seven Bucks Companies, in 2012 with the goal of building an entertainment brand. Focusing on ideas of "innovation, authenticity, and positive change," the brand has branched out into Seven Bucks Productions (parting ways with management company Principato-Young in 2019) and Seven Bucks Creative, a full-service ad agency. Seven Bucks Digital Studios, which finished the online store, came off in 2018 with his own YouTube channel, years later than it was planned. As of October 2021, Johnson has 190 million followers on Instagram, 16 million followers on TikTok, and 15 million subscribers to his YouTube channel. He held late-comedian John Witherspoon in high esteem.

American actor and producer Dwayne Johnson regularly posts promotional content. He has a lot of "strategic mutualism." He has endorsed: "Dish is the only place where you can find all the free care with qualified car stereo in the dad-cave" and "Turkey did a sex tape and she's fine" and "I rarely kept in touch with that crazy dry-cleaning couple, but I hope they went bankrupt five years ago." Johnson's father passed in 2020. Dwayne Johnson confirmed the positive COVID-19 test of his wife and kids on the Today (U.S. TV program) Show. Johnson decided to start the project only on the condition that he would be included in Fast Five and changed the character's name from Wilton "Scorpion King" Cruise to Luke Hobbs. The distributor focused on getting Johnson to support the movie, incorporating Johnson's action scenes into Peter Berg's Battleship (film).

Ten-year-old Johnson, who knows little about wrestling, was horrified by his father's portrayal of Richie "The Assassin" played by his grandfather, WWE Hall of Famer Peter Maivia. Dwayne Johnson's content turned into a WWF dose of the "Rock" before he achieved his dream of becoming a professional wrestler. Dwayne Johnson Financial Services were pivotal in negotiating TV deals and dictating a larger share of the profit for the WWF wrestlers. Johnson's agency auto-recorded its career. By the 2000s, Johnson's exposure had diminished. Dwayne Johnson, as "Rocky Maivia" at that time, was the first third-generation professional wrestler in the company, the "Dynamic Royal Rumble 1997." Seven Bucks Digital Studios, who had intended to launch a YouTube channel since 2013, were delayed to launch their channel in 2015. As of February 15, 2021, the channel has 5.6 million subscribers.

CHAPTER 6

Philanthropy and Social Impact

Forbes magazine has named Johnson as the top social media influencer as of 2016, and Dwayne Johnson has used his immense follower base to raise awareness of charitable causes and relief efforts around the world. Johnson has also demonstrated the leadership skills that he honed for years behind the scenes of the wrestling arena as a cast member of the HBO show "Ballers" and the host of "The Titan Games." Fans should remain engaged with Johnson's exploits in the entertainment world. Johnson continues to expand his work in a wide variety of media, including hosting documentaries, developing feature films, and producing projects covering topics like the life of entrepreneur Madame C.J. Walker, an exploration of Hawaii's rich cultural history, and the stories of passionate athletes. But it seems that Johnson may have other plans as well, and a political future for him is not out of the question: As of May 2022, fans were calling for him to run for President of the United States.

Before embarking on his career, Johnson has made a living out of social advocacy. Over the years, Johnson has become a highly sought-after public speaker and has been a fierce advocate for the causes close to his heart. For example, in 2017, Dwayne Johnson raised awareness on Instagram of the damage hurricanes Harvey and Irma did to the United States and surrounding territories. In 2006, Johnson founded the Dwayne Johnson Rock Foundation, a charity with interests in children's health. It has also made numerous contributions to the Make-A-Wish Foundation and the United Service Organizations, Inc. (USO). In 2017, he also told W magazine that he had run his own "undercover Mother Teresa operation." In the podcast "What Really Happened?," Johnson attempted to climb Mount Everest for charity in 2019.

CHAPTER 7

Conclusion

To the public and to his many fans, Dwayne 'The Rock' Johnson and the characters he plays in movies seem to radiate an inherent 'goodness.' In a verse, the essay beautifully summarizes Johnson's acts of kindness and the way he uses his wealth and privilege to help others. Reading this concluding piece made me stop and think about Johnson's inspiring legacy, and I had to agree with the essay when it observed that 'whether it lies on the wrestling mat or the silver screen, the legacy of The Rock has left quite the impression—developing over time into an intriguing narrative of its own.' But, this narrative is one that is not finished being written, due in part to Johnson's relentless work ethic and his refusal to be victim to any one stereotype. At the beginning of this essay, I noted that for his many years of trials and triumphs, Johnson is a figure who needs no introduction. I hope that the aforementioned analysis of the micro and megastages of his career has given readers a greater level of respect and admiration for the man who started off his journey being billed only as a third-generation wrestler.

Dwayne Johnson's journey from wrestling ring to movie star indeed says as much about reflection of his enduring popularity with new and established audiences alike. In the pro wrestling world, his invitation by fans to 'bring back his catch phrases' was viewed as a new star being created. Johnson is credited for his professional wrestling work for creating a 'larger-than-life, almost comic book superhero' figure for wrestling fans. Today, when his films arrive in theaters, he is known the world over and his rebooting characters reflect movies that emphasize 'his work as a bigger-than-life, action movie star committed to the genres and images that made him famous.' With multiple movies being released annually and many more to come, Johnson's legendary career would seem to be far from being completed.